Are We at the Park Yet?

by Rachel Russ
illustrated by Sofia Cardoso

Arthur, Lara and Dad are going to the park.

They get in the car.

Dad sets the map.

Dad waits. He turns right.

Is that
the park?

No, that is not the park.
It is the pool.

Dad turns right at the lights.

It is not the park!
It is a farm.

Dad turns into the road.

Cartoon
This is not the park!

Can we see the cartoon?
Yes, we can go and see it!

Dad gets popcorn for Arthur and Lara.

They all see the cartoon.

Dad, this is such fun!
The cartoon finishes.

We need to
get back soon.

Can we get back?
turn right
Dad cannot turn right!

Look Back

Encourage students to use the pictures to retell the story.